TEN EASY STEPS
To A Perfect Resume

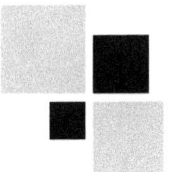

Carolyn Thompson

Let's face it; no one can write your resume like you can. Oh, sure, you can pay someone a lot of money to make it look beautiful and ensure it is grammatically correct, but in today's competitive job search industry, your resume needs to be sent electronically so paying for fancy paper or a portfolio-style resume is a thing of the past. Besides, paying someone else to write it may prove you don't have the computer skills necessary to compete in today's technology-focused work environment. At the end of the day, only you really know the work you have done. Even more importantly, only you know the work you want to do. How to translate that into an accurate, concise resume is the tough part.

No matter what your level of experience, this guide will give you the step-by-step instructions necessary to pull together a great resume. You can continually update your resume as your career progresses. The content will change over time as your career grows and evolves but, rest assured, following this easy format will make the initial process painless and updating a breeze.

The entire process of laying out your resume should not take more than a couple of hours.

STEP ONE:

KEEP YOUR LAYOUT SIMPLE AND MAKE SURE YOUR CONTACT INFORMATION IS ACCURATE AND CORRECT.

Sounds easy enough, but the most common errors on resumes are not in the body of the resume; they are in the contact information in the header.

Modern technology has opened up many opportunities for finding jobs, but the receiver on the other end of your carefully crafted cover letter and resume submittal is usually an e-mail parser. Parsing is a term that refers to the software technology that reads the information on your resume and adds it to a database so that the reviewer/s at the company can access it later.

It's best NOT to use a template for creating your resume. Templates can be difficult to expand upon later. As newer versions of software emerge, the template format you choose may not transfer well, which will require you to retype the entire document at a later date. Parsing technology can also have a hard time reading templates in the correct order. Parsing errors such as number transposition, saving your last name as your first name, and misidentification of your job title can create problems for the resume reviewer. Should your resume load into the system incorrectly, you won't receive an invitation for a job interview; nobody reviewed your resume because it was in an "unreadable/error" bin. If the system can't read the resume, it stores it in an "unreadable" area that is rarely accessed.

Except in a creative field, where you get extra points for creativity, parsing technology cannot read fancy fonts, graphics, or photos that you might feel compelled to add.

Microsoft Word is the best format to send a resume in. It's the easiest format for all computer systems to read. There is no need for colors or fancy fonts; just choose one that you like that is easy to read like Arial or Times New Roman. DO NOT SEND YOUR RESUME IN A PDF. This will ensure that your resume goes into the "error" bin, as parsing technology cannot read PDFs.

When you are ready to begin typing, open your Word document and put your name, address, contact phone, and e-mail at the top of the resume. You can center it, left or right justify, whatever you want, but don't worry about bolding or anything at this point...we are just getting the content together first.

STEP ONE:
CONTACT INFO – KEEP IT SIMPLE AND ACCURATE

Susie Smith
555 Any Street
Anytown, USA 00000
(555) 555-5555
Susie_Smith@whateveremail.com

Use a professional-sounding personal e-mail address on your resume. DO NOT use a company e-mail address on your resume...or an e-mail address that has anything catchy or personal in it. Yahoo, Hotmail, and Gmail are all free for basic e-mail, which is all you need for a job search. It's worth the investment to upgrade your storage space for these e-mail accounts to keep track of your sent e-mails. but you can also track your activities by printing them out and keeping them in a folder or even setting up a spreadsheet or database.

Make sure you have a daytime contact number. Most people use a cell phone or a home phone for contact numbers, and you can put both on the resume if you want, but a cell phone number is plenty. Hiring authorities don't work in the evenings. While it might be more convenient for you to talk in the evening, they work during the day and they are going to call you during the day. There is no harm in returning their calls at your convenience. You can leave your cell phone in the off position so it is not ringing at work and return those calls during your lunch hour.

Now that you've typed your contact info, MAKE SURE YOU PROOFREAD IT FOR ACCURACY!!

STEP TWO:

ADD THE COMPANIES YOU HAVE WORKED FOR AND THE DATES YOU WORKED THERE.

Most companies prefer chronological resumes, not functional ones, even at the executive level. The higher up the corporate ladder you go, the more concisely you need to communicate, no matter what your industry. A chronological resume is a safe bet regardless of your audience or your level of experience.

Start with the companies you worked for and the dates you worked there. Do not list supervisors, salaries, or reference phone numbers on your resume. Most employers prefer to see the actual months you worked for companies so if you can recall them, include the information. Putting the city and state is also a good idea.

If you held more than one position at a company, you should break down the jobs you had there by title and the dates you had them, indicating progression, promotion, and additional expertise.

If you had more than a couple of positions at one company, detail the most recent five years. Providing a simple listing with a brief description of the earlier jobs is appropriate, particularly if they show a career progression of promotion.

It's customary to put the most recent job first, as most companies are going to look at what you have done in the past five years as a real indicator of your knowledge, skills, and abilities. You can deviate from this format if you are re-entering the workforce after taking time off or if you have made some sort of major career change, but that is rare. In these cases, you should highlight the relevant experience you intend to utilize as the most recent work notated with appropriate dates. If you have long, explainable gaps such as sabbaticals, time off to start a family or to care for an ill family member, etc. you should insert that information if you feel it's relevant and you are comfortable talking about it in an interview. It's always best to fill in the blanks for reviewers so they can better understand your experience.

STEP TWO:
ADD COMPANIES AND DATES

Susie Smith
555 Any Street
Anytown, USA 00000
(555) 555-5555
Susie_Smith@whateveremail.com

1/2007–present
ABC Company, Anytown, USA
Manager 1/2008–present
Senior Associate 1/2007–1/2008

5/2004–12/2006
XYZ Partners, Anytown, USA
Senior Associate 8/2005–12/2006
Staff Associate 5/2004–7/2005

5/2002–4/2004
123 Incorporated, New Town, USA
Staff Associate 9/2002–4/2004
Intern 5/2002–8/2002

STEP THREE:

ADD A QUICK DESCRIPTION
OF THE COMPANY.

After you have gotten the dates and titles documented, it's a really good idea to write a quick description of the company, even if you feel it's a well-known company. This is particularly important if you move from one city to another. Employers in the new city may not have any earthly idea what ABC or XYZ did, even though it was a premier employer in your old hometown.

Companies get bought out, change names, and evolve over time. It's important that, as these changes occur, you make note of it on your resume.

One sentence is adequate but it should contain some indication of company size, location, industry, ownership (publicly traded or privately held), number of employees, annual revenues, etc. For example, if you are in nursing, you might note how large the hospital is by the number of beds, whether it's a private hospital or part of a large corporation, and whether or not it's a specialty hospital.

STEP THREE:
ADD A COMPANY DESCRIPTION

Susie Smith
555 Any Street
Anytown, USA 00000
(555) 555-5555
Susie_Smith@whateveremail.com

1/2007–present
ABC Company, Anytown, USA
ABC Company is a $2B publicly traded international manufacturing company.

Manager 1/2008–present
Senior Associate 1/2007–1/2008

5/2004–12/2006
XYZ Partners, Anytown, USA
XYZ Partners is a privately held company with 2,000 employees in six states.

Senior Associate 8/2005–12/2006
Staff Associate 5/2004–7/2005

5/2002–4/2004
123 Incorporated, New Town, USA
123 Incorporated was a small company that was subsequently bought out by 789 Corporation.

Staff Associate 9/2002–4/2004
Intern 5/2002–8/2002

STEP FOUR:

ADD YOUR JOB DESCRIPTIONS.

Ask yourself: What were my responsibilities in each job? More importantly though, what do you want to continue to do?

Your resume is meant to be an accurate representation of your skills and abilities and what experiences you intend to carry forward to your next position. You do not need to include everything you have ever done. Most employers are looking for what you have done in the last five years as an accurate representation of what you can do for them. If you had duties or were responsible for things in the past that you did not enjoy and do not want to do in the future, minimize the discussion of those duties and do not highlight them for others to take notice of.

Employers want to know where you have worked, what kinds of companies they were, and what you did there. There is a difference between your job responsibilities and what you accomplished in your jobs. Do not copy a company-written job description on your resume. Talk about volume of work you were responsible for, such as sales or revenue responsibility, or number of offices/employees, etc. you serviced or managed. Include any technical experience you have that is pertinent to your industry and role. Whether you are a CFO or an entry-level person, details are really important. Your ability to describe your duties is a test of your ability to communicate in writing, so use action words and write a little paragraph about each job with just a few sentences:

Managers: Supervised XX people in $$ division of XXX corporation with $$$ in revenue. Reported to (title). Responsibilities included preparation of management reports, working with peers in other divisions on cross-functional teams, and approval of all travel and training expenses for division.

Staff employees: Performed XX duties in $$ division/department of XX corporation. Responsibilities included daily recording of activities, working with team members on projects relating to overall goals of department and company. Worked directly with managers on any discrepancies or escalations as necessary.

STEP FOUR:
ADD YOUR JOB DESCRIPTIONS

Susie Smith
555 Any Street
Anytown, USA 00000
(555) 555-5555
Susie_Smith@whateveremail.com

1/2007–present
ABC Company, Anytown, USA
ABC Company is a $2B publicly traded international manufacturing company.

Division Manager 1/2008–present
Manage staff of five in the domestic distribution division, a $500M division. Report to divisional director. Responsibilities include hiring, training, and mentoring of staff in accordance with company guidelines. Maintain divisional reporting and ensure timely reporting to corporate.

Senior Associate 1/2007–1/2008
Responsibilities included monitoring the activities of the distribution center including production, error reporting, and quality control activities. Reported to division manager and was promoted into that position after the manager's departure.
5/2004–12/2006
XYZ Partners, Anytown, USA

XYZ Partners is a privately held company with 2,000 employees in six states.

Senior Associate 8/2005–12/2006
Responsibilities included assisting in training and supervision of three staff associates performing word processing and proofreading as assigned. Ensured that quality control guidelines and project deadlines were being met. Reported to senior manager of production.

Staff Associate 5/2004–7/2005
Received job-specific training on document control and word processing as required by diverse clientele. Position required attention to detail, accuracy, and strong computer skills in Word. Reported to senior associate and was subsequently promoted into that role.

5/2002–4/2004
123 Incorporated, New Town, USA
123 Incorporated was a small company that was subsequently bought out by 789 Corporation.

Staff Associate 9/2002–4/2004
Worked on a variety of projects as assigned using Excel, Word, and database research. Liaised with management and clients regarding content-related issues and supervised interns performing basic Internet research.

Intern 5/2002–8/2002
Performed basic Internet research as assigned by staff associates.

STEP FIVE:

ADD YOUR ACCOMPLISHMENTS.

There is a big difference between what the company has hired you to do and what you individually accomplish in each job compared to your peers.

Go back to each job and think about what you made, saved, or achieved in this position. What did you contribute that set you apart from your peers? How did you make your company more profitable? How did you contribute to better efficiencies within your group? What special awards did you receive? Why was your work there important?

The easiest way to add these is to bullet point one or two measurable accomplishments in each job under your descriptions. Be specific about the value of those accomplishments to the company and your involvement in them. Your ability to distinguish your responsibilities and accomplishments is what sets you apart from your competition. Don't be afraid to be proud of what you accomplished beyond what they hired you to do.

STEP FIVE:
ADD YOUR ACCOMPLISHMENTS

Susie Smith
555 Any Street
Anytown, USA 00000
(555) 555-5555
Susie_Smith@whateveremail.com

1/2007–present
ABC Company, Anytown, USA
ABC Company is a $2B publicly traded international manufacturing company.

Division Manager 1/2008–present
Manage staff of five in the domestic distribution division, a $500M division. Report to divisional director. Responsibilities include hiring, training and mentoring of staff in accordance with company guidelines. Maintain divisional reporting and ensure timely reporting to corporate.
- Received "Top Performance Award 2007" for suggesting and implementing a new procedure that saved the company over $15,000 in printing costs.
- Implemented new employee referral program and reduced turnover to less than 10% in under six months.

Senior Associate 1/2007–1/2008
Responsibilities included monitoring the activities of the distribution center including production, error reporting, and quality control activities. Reported to division manager and was promoted into that position after the manager's departure.
- Was selected as "Associate of the Month" four times in 2007

5/2004–12/2006
XYZ Partners, Anytown, USA
XYZ Partners is a privately held company with 2,000 employees in six states.

Senior Associate 8/2005–12/2006
Responsibilities included assisting in training and supervision of three staff associates performing word processing and proofreading as assigned. Ensured quality control guidelines and project deadlines were being met. Reported to senior manager of production.
- Was chosen to work on prestigious project for member of Congress requiring security and background screening.

Staff Associate 5/2004–7/2005
Received job-specific training on document control and word processing as required by diverse clientele. Position required attention to detail, accuracy, and strong computer skills using Word. Reported to senior associate and was promoted into that role.
- Discovered and corrected major data entry error that ultimately made the database run twice as efficiently.

5/2002–4/2004
123 Incorporated, New Town, USA
123 Incorporated was a small company that was bought out by 789 Corporation in 2005.

Staff Associate 9/2002–4/2004
Worked on a variety of projects as assigned using Excel, Word, and database research. Liaised with management and clients regarding content-related issues and supervised interns performing basic Internet research.
- Was selected for company's employee activity committee.

Intern 5/2002–8/2002
Performed basic Internet research as assigned by staff associates.

STEP SIX:

FORMATTING THE PAGE.

At this point you are ready to start some formatting: bolding, underlining, etc.

As for the text, a 9, 10, 11 or 12-pt typeface is fine, but now that you have a lot of great content, you need to make it jump off the page. Pay attention to consistency in formatting, meaning if you underline dates or bold the job titles, you need to be consistent on the page and underline or bold all of them. Also, if you make changes or additions later, pay attention to tenses in your job descriptions. Only the current job should be written in the present tense. All your previous jobs should be in past tense.

Keep your resume to two pages. Five years of work experience for each page is a good rule of thumb. If your professional experience is longer than that, a statement at the end of the resume such as "References and work experience prior to XX date available upon request" is appropriate. Just make sure you have that addendum prepared in case anyone asks for it. If your resume is three pages long try using a smaller font. You can also easily adjust the page margins to add more room to each page; just make sure you work within the printable area of the page.

STEP SIX:
FORMATTING THE PAGE

Susie Smith
555 Any Street
Anytown, USA 00000
(555) 555-5555
Susie_Smith@whateveremail.com

1/2007–present
ABC Company, Anytown, USA
ABC Company is a $2B publicly traded international manufacturing company.

Division Manager 1/2008–present
Manage staff of five in the domestic distribution division, a $500M division. Report to divisional director. Responsibilities include hiring, training, and mentoring of staff in accordance with company guidelines. Maintain divisional reporting and ensure timely reporting to corporate.
- Received "Top Performance Award 2007" for suggesting and implementing a new procedure that saved the company over $15,000 in printing costs.
- Implemented new employee referral program and reduced turnover to less than 10% in under six months.

Senior Associate 1/2007-1/2008
Responsibilities included monitoring the activities of the distribution center including production, error reporting and quality control activities. Reported to division manager and was promoted into that position after the manager's departure.
- Was selected as "Associate of the Month" four times in 2007

5/2004–12/2006
XYZ Partners, Anytown, USA
XYZ Partners is a privately held company with 2,000 employees in six states.

Senior Associate 8/2005–12/2006
Responsibilities included assisting in training and supervision of three staff associates performing word processing and proofreading as assigned. Ensured quality control guidelines and project deadlines were being met. Reported to senior manager of production.
- Was chosen to work on prestigious project for member of Congress requiring security and background screening.

Staff Associate 5/2004–7/2005
Received job-specific training on document control and word processing as required by diverse clientele. Position required attention to detail, accuracy, and strong computer skills using Word. Reported to senior associate and was promoted into that role.
- Discovered and corrected major data entry error that ultimately made the database run twice as efficiently.

5/2002–4/2004
123 Incorporated, New Town, USA
123 Incorporated was a small company that was bought out by 789 Corporation in 2005.

Staff Associate 9/2002–4/2004
Worked on a variety of projects as assigned using Excel, Word and database research. Liaised with management and clients regarding content-related issues and supervised interns performing basic Internet research.
- Was selected for company's employee activity committee.

Intern 5/2002–8/2002
Performed basic Internet research as assigned by staff associates.

Now it's starting to look like a real resume!

STEP SEVEN:

ADDING EDUCATION AND CERTIFICATIONS.

You can list your education first or last, just not in the middle!

The certifications you put forth should be only those that you need for the jobs you are applying for. For example, if you are the accounting manager looking for the controller job, but you sold real estate or dabbled as a financial planner in the past, those certifications are not required for the job you are applying for and should be left off your resume. Putting them in there will not make a good talking point as these are interests that you pursued in the past and are not relevant to the job at hand.

Education should start with the highest degree or accreditation, include the month and year you earned it, and work your way backward. You also want to include the city and state the college is in if you can since many state universities have multiple campuses but are all part of one university system. It makes it easier to verify your degrees if you give the proper information.

It's best if you give the full name of the university, not the name of the school within the university. For example, the Darden School of Business is at the University of Virginia. If you have a bachelor of science degree from the school within the university, your BS is from the University of Virginia.

If you earned an associate's degree and then went on to complete your bachelor's degree, it's not really necessary to put the associate's degree on your resume, unless it accounts for a gap in employment.

You can now add section headers to your resume for work experience, education, and certifications.

STEP SEVEN:
ADDING EDUCATION AND CERTIFICATIONS

Susie Smith
555 Any Street
Anytown, USA 00000
(555) 555-5555
Susie_Smith@whateveremail.com

WORK EXPERIENCE

1/2007–present
ABC Company, Anytown, USA
ABC Company is a $2B publicly traded international manufacturing company.

Division Manager 1/2008–present
Manage staff of five in the domestic distribution division, a $500M division. Report to divisional director. Responsibilities include hiring, training, and mentoring of staff in accordance with company guidelines. Maintain divisional reporting and ensure timely reporting to corporate.
- Received "Top Performance Award 2007" for suggesting and implementing a new procedure that saved the company over $15,000 in printing costs.
- Implemented new employee referral program and reduced turnover to less than 10% in under six months.

Senior Associate 1/2007–1/2008
Responsibilities included monitoring the activities of the distribution center including production, error reporting, and quality control activities. Reported to division manager and was promoted into that position after the manager's departure.
- Was selected as "Associate of the Month" four times in 2007

5/2004–12/2006
XYZ Partners, Anytown, USA
XYZ Partners is a privately held company with 2,000 employees in six states.

Senior Associate 8/2005–12/2006
Responsibilities included assisting in training and supervision of three staff associates performing word processing and proofreading as assigned. Ensured quality control guidelines and project deadlines were being met. Reported to senior manager of production.
- Was chosen to work on prestigious project for member of Congress requiring security and background screening.

Staff Associate 5/2004–7/2005
Received job-specific training on document control and word processing as required by diverse clientele. Position required attention to detail, accuracy, and strong computer skills using Word. Reported to senior associate and was promoted into that role.
- Discovered and corrected major data entry error that ultimately made the database run twice as efficiently.

5/2002–4/2004
123 Incorporated, New Town, USA
123 Incorporated was a small company that was bought out by 789 Corporation in 2005.

Staff Associate 9/2002–4/2004
Worked on a variety of projects as assigned using Excel, Word, and database research. Liaised with management and clients regarding content-related issues and supervised interns performing basic Internet research.
- Was selected for company's employee activity committee.

Intern 5/2002–8/2002
Performed basic Internet research as assigned by staff associates.

<u>EDUCATION AND CERTIFICATIONS</u>
BA – Management, American University, Washington, DC May 2002
Certified Management Accountant, IMA 2005

STEP EIGHT:

ADDING SKILLS.

Computer skills are a must no matter what your level or job. List them out rather than bury them in the job descriptions. It's easier for someone to read an inclusive list than to have to pull all the information from your narrative. Now, in some jobs it still may be appropriate to discuss the technical skills applied in the job description, but it would not be considered redundant to include them in their own section as well.

Before you finish this section, what do you think your list of skills is telling a potential employer? When you read that list, is the technology you are discussing current? If you think something in your list is outdated or has become stale, remove it. Recruiters do keyword searches on databases, so make sure if you want to work on SAP and you have that skill, that you list it.

Now, let's say you have worked in a small-company accounting department on QuickBooks, but now you want to work in a larger corporation. No major company uses that software for accounting, so if you state that you are an expert on QuickBooks, they will know you have only small-company accounting skills and will likely not choose you for an interview.

Will prospective employers be wowed by your list or is it a list they may pass over? Saying you know Microsoft Office is not the same as saying you are an advanced user of Word or an advanced user of Excel, including macros and pivot tables.

STEP EIGHT:
ADDING SKILLS

Susie Smith
555 Any Street
Anytown, USA 00000
(555) 555-5555
Susie_Smith@whateveremail.com

WORK EXPERIENCE

1/2007–present
ABC Company, Anytown, USA
ABC Company is a $2B publicly traded international manufacturing company.

Division Manager 1/2008–present
Manage staff of five in the domestic distribution division, a $500M division. Report to divisional director. Responsibilities include hiring, training and mentoring of staff in accordance with company guidelines. Maintain divisional reporting and ensure timely reporting to corporate.
- Received "Top Performance Award 2007" for suggesting and implementing a new procedure that saved the company over $15,000 in printing costs.
- Implemented new employee referral program and reduced turnover to less than 10% in under six months.

Senior Associate 1/2007–1/2008
Responsibilities included monitoring the activities of the distribution center including production, error reporting and quality control activities. Reported to Division Manager and was promoted into that position after the manager's departure.
- Was selected as "Associate of the Month" four times in 2007

5/2004–12/2006
XYZ Partners, Anytown, USA
XYZ Partners is a privately held company with 2,000 employees in six states.

Senior Associate 8/2005–12/2006
Responsibilities included assisting in training and supervision of three staff associates performing word processing and proofreading as assigned. Ensured quality control guidelines and project deadlines were being met. Reported to senior manager of production.
- Was chosen to work on prestigious project for member of Congress requiring security and background screening.

Staff Associate 5/2004–7/2005
Received job-specific training on document control and word processing as required by diverse clientele. Position required attention to detail, accuracy, and strong computer skills using Word. Reported to senior associate and was promoted into that role.
- Discovered and corrected major data entry error that ultimately made the database run twice as efficiently.

5/2002-4/2004
123 Incorporated, New Town, USA
123 Incorporated was a small company that was bought out by 789 Corporation in 2005.

Staff Associate 9/2002–4/2004
Worked on a variety of projects as assigned using Excel, Word, and database research. Liaised with management and clients regarding content-related issues and supervised interns performing basic Internet research.
- Was selected for company's employee activity committee.

Intern 5/2002–8/2002
Performed basic Internet research as assigned by staff associate

EDUCATION AND CERTIFICATIONS
BA – Management, American University, Washington, DC May 2002
Certified Management Accountant, IMA 2005

SKILLS
Oracle Sequel Query, Filenet, Premium Accounting System, Premium Audit Adjustment Module, and Premium Processing System; proficient with Microsoft Office 97 (Excel, Microsoft Word, Access Database), Lotus 1-2-3, and WordPerfect; excellent work ethic, communication skills, and interpersonal skills.

STEP NINE:

EVALUATE YOUR CONTENT
AND CREATE AN OBJECTIVE.

Before we move forward to finishing your resume and finding that great new job, MAKE SURE you are putting forth an accurate representation of your experience. Does it make sense to the audience? Sometimes the job titles a company gives you may not make sense to people outside your company. Titles such as associate I, associate II, analyst IV, and analyst V make sense to your employer's internal structure and org chart but not to anyone else outside the company.

How do you know if you need to change your job title on your resume? That's easy! Go look on the Internet and search for your job title to see who is advertising for it. After all the jobs at your company come up, is anyone else looking for a database administrator III? Perhaps senior database administrator is a more accurate reflection of the job you did. Try searching for that and you'll probably find a lot more postings.

As you are reading your new masterpiece, do you see things on there that you would not want to do again? Is experience lacking in the areas that you want to be involved in? Both of these questions are really important. Employers are looking for the experience they want on your resume. If it's there, they are going to call you about doing that work for them. If it's not there, they are not going to call you.

An objective statement is appropriate if you want to let people know what you are looking for. Short thumbnail summaries are also appropriate ways to convey soft skill information. Some people like to add keywords at the top, but if you wrote well-crafted job descriptions, as in STEP THREE, and you described the companies well, as in STEP TWO, and you have solid accomplishments from STEP FOUR, then all you may need is a clear statement of your objective.

Well, what if I want to do work that is the next step up from what I have done?

Easy, add it into your objective. Say you are an accounting manager and you want to be a controller next. You need to make sure the word "controller" appears on your resume. Remember the parsing technology? When you are evaluating your content, you need to think of key words, just like the job titles. If you are looking for a CFO role and have never done that, you need to make sure chief financial officer or CFO appears somewhere in your text.

Same would apply if you are trying to switch careers or you are re-entering the job market—you MUST have a statement of objectives. Why? Remember back at the beginning when I told you that employers are looking to hire people who have the exact job title and are proven in the specific role they are trying to fill? Well, if you are looking to make a strategic move, you need to let people know that.

One note on trying to get promoted into the next job: it's a lot easier to get promoted at your current company than to expect a new company to hire you into a higher-level role. Most employers want tried-and-true proven experience and will choose someone who already has that job title on the resume over someone who does not, unless you come highly recommended. So, what's the lesson here? Put it in your objective, but network hard to find a job that someone will recommend you for.

An objective statement is also really helpful if you are looking to relocate from another part of the country. Most recruiters will not consider out-of-town candidates unless they have a high-paying job that will offer relocation. If you are moving because you are getting married, etc., you can note that in your e-mail, cover letter, or a carefully crafted objective statement.

Hopefully, the end reader will see the skills and abilities he or she needs for the job in the resume and give you a call!

STEP NINE:
EVALUATE CONTENT AND CREATE AN OBJECTIVE

Susie Smith
555 Any Street
Anytown, USA 00000
(555) 555-5555
Susie_Smith@whateveremail.com

OBJECTIVE
To find a position in management that offers a wide variety of challenges and responsibilities in a major corporation.

WORK EXPERIENCE

1/2007–present
ABC Company, Anytown, USA
ABC Company is a $2B publicly traded international manufacturing company.

Division Manager 1/2008–present
Manage staff of five in the domestic distribution division, a $500M division. Report to divisional director. Responsibilities include hiring, training and mentoring of staff in accordance with company guidelines. Maintain divisional reporting and ensure timely reporting to corporate.
- Received "Top Performance Award 2007" for suggesting and implementing a new procedure that saved the company over $15,000 in printing costs.
- Implemented new employee referral program and reduced turnover to less than 10% in under six months.

Senior Associate 1/2007–1/2008
Responsibilities included monitoring the activities of the distribution center including production, error reporting and quality control activities. Reported to Division Manager and was promoted into that position after the manager's departure.
- Was selected as "Associate of the Month" four times in 2007

5/2004–12/2006
XYZ Partners, Anytown, USA
XYZ Partners is a privately held company with 2,000 employees in six states.

Senior Associate 8/2005–12/2006

Responsibilities included assisting in training and supervision of three staff associates performing word processing and proofreading as assigned. Ensured quality control guidelines and project deadlines were being met. Reported to senior manager of production.

- Was chosen to work on prestigious project for member of Congress requiring security and background screening.

Staff Associate 5/2004–7/2005

Received job-specific training on document control and word processing as required by diverse clientele. Position required attention to detail, accuracy, and strong computer skills using Word. Reported to senior associate and was promoted into that role.

- Discovered and corrected major data entry error that ultimately made the database run twice as efficiently.

5/2002–4/2004

123 Incorporated, New Town, USA

123 Incorporated was a small company that was bought out by 789 Corporation in 2005.

Staff Associate 9/2002–4/2004

Worked on a variety of projects as assigned using Excel, Word, and database research. Liaised with management and clients regarding content-related issues and supervised interns performing basic Internet research.

- Was selected for company's employee activity committee.

Intern 5/2002–8/2002

Performed basic Internet research as assigned by staff associate

EDUCATION AND CERTIFICATIONS

BA – Management, American University, Washington, DC May 2002
Certified Management Accountant, IMA 2005

SKILLS

Oracle Sequel Query, Filenet, Premium Accounting System, Premium Audit Adjustment Module, and Premium

Processing System; proficient with Microsoft Office 97 (Excel, Microsoft Word, Access Database), Lotus 1-2-3, and WordPerfect; excellent work ethic, communication skills, and interpersonal skills.

STEP TEN:

PROOFREAD YOUR COMPLETED CONTENT.

First two words: SPELL CHECK!

Take a break, and then reread what you wrote.

Are your descriptions interesting to read? Do they tell a story? Did you use enough action words? If you used full sentences you have already used nouns and verbs...so you probably did OK here. Is your resume an honest reflection of your experience?

Now, here comes the part where you have to step back and take a hard, objective look at your content and answer two questions:

1) Does the job title I am looking to gain appear on my resume somewhere?
2) Does my resume reflect the experience, skills, and abilities that employers describe in the job postings I am responding to?

These are the two most important questions you need to be able to answer yes to. This will ensure you land the interviews you want for the job you are really seeking. To double-check, you can refer to your Internet research, paying attention to the phraseology used in the descriptions. You want your resume to be attractive to these people and it's worth the effort to make it read the way they want it to read.

Recruiters do KEYWORD searches to pull resumes out of online resume databases like CareerBuilder and Monster. You have to make sure that you are using keywords in your resume so it will appear on search lists. One strategy that also adds to the number of times your resume will be viewed is to add a string of keywords in the footer of your document, in white font; they don't print out but the databases will still read them.

Recruiters and hiring managers get thousands of submissions from all over the world for postings they put on the Internet.

Some commonsense things you need to know about the resume review process:

- Recruiters and hiring managers are often looking just as much for reasons NOT TO call you as they are for reasons TO call you, because they get so many resumes. So the more in line your resume is with the job descriptions, the better your chances are of getting an interview. They get so many responses that they have to be highly selective about the candidates they bring in; if your resume is not in line with the job description, they are not going to call you.

- Resume reviewers often don't read the cover letter first. They look at the resume first, and then maybe the e-mail or cover letter you sent for salary information or something additional that perhaps their ad asked for. It doesn't matter what you write—they will read it after they are interested in your resume.

- Attaching the cover letter to the resume and submitting it as the first page of your resume document only messes with the parsing technology so it really is a waste of time. Your cover letter or e-mail should be short, sweet, and to the point if you are sending one. Attention to detail here is key as most people will toss it out if you refer to the wrong job title or description, or address it to the wrong party...which happens ALL the time!

- You should not include photographs or videos with your resume submissions unless you are an actor, television personality, or the position requires it. You should not send portfolios or writing samples unless they are requested.

- Have you "Googled" yourself lately? Prospective employers will. Taking time to make sure you have a professional Internet appearance is as important as shining your shoes, or getting a new suit and a haircut before the interview. YouTube postings, MySpace pages, personal Web sites, blogs, and other references to your name should be G-rated, positive reflections of who you are as a professional.

Those college photos or other candid pics you may have previously posted for your friends and family to see should be removed while you are looking for a job.

Now that you have a PERFECT RESUME, go out and get the job you want and deserve! You can play with the fonts, add lines, etc. to make your resume more unique if you want to. Some examples of how that might look follow here as well as a five-year update to the sample resume.

Should you need any additional interview tips or suggestions, feel free to visit my company's Web site www.cm-cs.com. They are posted under the "FOR CANDIDATES" tab. You will also find a link there called "Asked and Answered" where you can submit any resume preparation, interview etiquette, or other job-search-related question directly to me and my staff. With over twenty years of recruiting experience, we are happy to help you any way we can.

SAMPLE RESUMES AND UPDATE EXAMPLE

Version 1 Resume

SUSIE SMITH

555 Any Street
Anytown, USA 00000
(555) 555-5555
Susie_Smith@whateveremail.com

OBJECTIVE

To find a position in management that offers a wide variety of challenges and responsibilities in a major corporation.

WORK EXPERIENCE

1/2007–present
ABC Company, Anytown, USA
ABC Company is a $2B publicly traded international manufacturing company.

Division Manager 1/2008–present
Manage staff of five in the domestic distribution division, a $500M division. Report to divisional director. Responsibilities include hiring, training, and mentoring of staff in accordance with company guidelines. Maintain divisional reporting and ensure timely reporting to corporate.
- Received "Top Performance Award 2007" for suggesting and implementing a new procedure that saved the company over $15,000 in printing costs.
- Implemented new employee referral program and reduced turnover to less than 10% in under six months.

Senior Associate 1/2007–1/2008
Responsibilities included monitoring the activities of the distribution center including production, error reporting, and quality control activities. Reported to division manager and was promoted into that position after the manager's departure.
- Was selected as "Associate of the Month" four times in 2007

5/2004–12/2006
XYZ Partners, Anytown, USA
XYZ Partners is a privately held company with 2,000 employees in six states.

Senior Associate 8/2005–12/2006

Responsibilities included assisting in training and supervision of three staff associates performing word processing and proofreading as assigned. Ensured quality control guidelines and project deadlines were being met. Reported to senior manager of production.

- Was chosen to work on prestigious project for member of Congress requiring security and background screening.

Staff Associate 5/2004–7/2005

Received job-specific training on document control and word processing as required by diverse clientele. Position required attention to detail, accuracy, and strong computer skills in Word. Reported to senior associate and was promoted into that role.

- Discovered and corrected major data entry error that ultimately made the database run twice as efficiently.

5/2002–4/2004

123 Incorporated, New Town, USA

123 Incorporated was a small company that was bought out by 789 Corporation in 2005.

Staff Associate 9/2002–4/2004

Worked on a variety of projects as assigned using Excel, Word, and database research. Liaised with management and clients regarding content-related issues and supervised interns performing basic Internet research.

- Was selected for company's employee activity committee.

Intern 5/2002–8/2002

Performed basic Internet research as assigned by staff associates.

EDUCATION AND CERTIFICATIONS

BA – Management, American University, Washington, DC May 2002
Certified Management Accountant, IMA 2005

SKILLS

Oracle Sequel Query, Filenet, Premium Accounting System, Premium Audit Adjustment Module, and Premium Processing System; proficient with Microsoft Office 97 (Excel, Microsoft Word, Access Database), Lotus 1-2-3, and WordPerfect; excellent work ethic, communication skills, and interpersonal skills.

Version 2 Resume

Susie Smith

555 Any Street
Anytown, USA 00000
(555) 555-5555
Susie_Smith@whateveremail.com

OBJECTIVE

To find a position in management that offers a wide variety of challenges and responsibilities in a major corporation.

WORK EXPERIENCE

1/2007–present ABC Company, Anytown, USA
ABC Company is a $2B publicly traded international manufacturing company.

Division Manager 1/2008–present
Manage staff of five in the domestic distribution division, a $500M division. Report to divisional director. Responsibilities include hiring, training, and mentoring of staff in accordance with company guidelines. Maintain divisional reporting and ensure timely reporting to corporate.

- Received "Top Performance Award 2007" for suggesting and implementing a new procedure that saved the company over $15,000 in printing costs.
- Implemented new employee referral program and reduced turnover to less than 10% in under six months.

Senior Associate 1/2007–1/2008
Responsibilities included monitoring the activities of the distribution center including production, error reporting, and quality control activities. Reported to division manager and was promoted into that position after the manager's departure.

- Was selected as "Associate of the Month" four times in 2007

5/2004–12/2006 XYZ Partners, Anytown, USA
XYZ Partners is a privately held company with 2,000 employees in six states.

Senior Associate 8/2005–12/2006
Responsibilities included assisting in training and supervision of three staff

associates performing word processing and proofreading as assigned. Ensured quality control guidelines and project deadlines were being met. Reported to senior manager of production.
- Was chosen to work on prestigious project for member of Congress requiring security and background screening.

Staff Associate 5/2004–7/2005
Received job-specific training on document control and word processing as required by diverse clientele. Position required attention to detail, accuracy, and strong computer skills using Word. Reported to senior associate and was promoted into that role.
- Discovered and corrected major data entry error that ultimately made the database run twice as efficiently.

5/2002–4/2004   123 Incorporated, New Town, USA
123 Incorporated was a small company that was bought out by 789 Corporation in 2005.

Staff Associate 9/2002–4/2004
Worked on a variety of projects as assigned using Excel, Word, and database research. Liaised with management and clients regarding content-related issues and supervised interns performing basic Internet research.
- Was selected for company's employee activity committee.

Intern 5/2002–8/2002
Performed basic Internet research as assigned by staff associates.

EDUCATION AND CERTIFICATIONS

BA – Management, American University, Washington, DC May 2002
Certified Management Accountant, IMA 2005

SKILLS

Oracle Sequel Query, Filenet, Premium Accounting System, Premium Audit Adjustment Module, and Premium Processing System; proficient with Microsoft Office 97 (Excel, Microsoft Word, Access Database), Lotus 1-2-3, and WordPerfect; excellent work ethic, communication skills, and interpersonal skills.

Version 3 Resume

Susie Smith

555 Any Street, Anytown, USA 00000
Ph (555) 555-5555 e-mail: Susie_Smith@whateveremail.com

OBJECTIVE

To find a position in management that offers a wide variety of challenges and responsibilities in a major corporation.

WORK EXPERIENCE

1/2007–present
ABC Company, Anytown, USA
ABC Company is a $2B publicly traded international manufacturing company.

Division Manager 1/2008–present
Manage staff of five in the domestic distribution division, a $500M division. Report to divisional director. Responsibilities include hiring, training, and mentoring of staff in accordance with company guidelines. Maintain divisional reporting and ensure timely reporting to corporate.

- Received "Top Performance Award 2007" for suggesting and implementing a new procedure that saved the company over $15,000 in printing costs.
- Implemented new employee referral program and reduced turnover to less than 10% in under six months.

Senior Associate 1/2007–1/2008
Responsibilities included monitoring the activities of the distribution center including production, error reporting, and quality control activities. Reported to division manager and was promoted into that position after the manager's departure.

- Was selected as "Associate of the Month" four times in 2007

5/2004–12/2006
XYZ Partners, Anytown, USA
XYZ Partners is a privately held company with 2,000 employees in six states.

Senior Associate 8/2005–12/2006
Responsibilities included assisting in training and supervision of three staff associates performing word processing and proofreading as assigned. Ensured

quality control guidelines and project deadlines were being met. Reported to senior manager of production.

- Was chosen to work on prestigious project for member of Congress requiring security and background screening.

Staff Associate 5/2004–7/2005
Received job-specific training on document control and word processing as required by diverse clientele. Position required attention to detail, accuracy and strong computer skills using Word. Reported to senior associate and was promoted into that role.

- Discovered and corrected major data entry error that ultimately made the database run twice as efficiently.

5/2002–4/2004
123 Incorporated, New Town, USA
123 Incorporated was a small company that was bought out by 789 Corporation in 2005.
Staff Associate 9/2002–4/2004
Worked on a variety of projects as assigned using Excel, Word, and database research. Liaised with management and clients regarding content-related issues and supervised interns performing basic Internet research.

- Was selected for company's employee activity committee.

Intern 5/2002–8/2002
Performed basic Internet research as assigned by staff associates.

EDUCATION AND CERTIFICATIONS

BA – Management, American University, Washington, DC May 2002
Certified Management Accountant, IMA 2005

SKILLS

Oracle Sequel Query, Filenet, Premium Accounting System, Premium Audit Adjustment Module, and Premium Processing System; proficient with Microsoft Office 97 (Excel, Microsoft Word, Access Database), Lotus 1-2-3, and WordPerfect; excellent work ethic, communication skills, and interpersonal skills.

Version 4 Resume

SUSIE SMITH

555 Any Street, Anytown, USA 00000
Ph (555) 555-5555 e-mail: Susie_Smith@whateveremail.com

OBJECTIVE

To find a position in management that offers a wide variety of challenges and responsibilities in a major corporation.

WORK EXPERIENCE

1/2007–PRESENT
ABC COMPANY, ANYTOWN, USA
ABC Company is a $2B publicly traded international manufacturing company.

DIVISION MANAGER 1/2008–PRESENT

Manage staff of five in the domestic distribution division, a $500M division. Report to divisional director. Responsibilities include hiring, training, and mentoring of staff in accordance with company guidelines. Maintain divisional reporting and ensure timely reporting to corporate.

- Received "Top Performance Award 2007" for suggesting and implementing a new procedure that saved the company over $15,000 in printing costs.
- Implemented new employee referral program and reduced turnover to less than 10% in under six months.

SENIOR ASSOCIATE 1/2007–1/2008

Responsibilities included monitoring the activities of the distribution center including production, error reporting, and quality control activities. Reported to division manager and was promoted into that position after the manager's departure.

- Was selected as "Associate of the Month" four times in 2007

5/2004-12/2006
XYZ PARTNERS, ANYTOWN, USA
XYZ Partners is a privately held company with 2,000 employees in six states.

SENIOR ASSOCIATE 8/2005–12/2006

Responsibilities included assisting in training and supervision of three staff associates performing word processing and proofreading as assigned. Ensured

quality control guidelines and project deadlines were being met. Reported to senior manager of production.
- Was chosen to work on prestigious project for member of Congress requiring security and background screening.

STAFF ASSOCIATE 5/2004–7/2005

Received job-specific training on document control and word processing as required by diverse clientele. Position required attention to detail, accuracy, and strong computer skills using Word. Reported to senior associate and was promoted into that role.
- Discovered and corrected major data entry error that ultimately made the database run twice as efficiently.

5/2002–4/2004
123 INCORPORATED, NEW TOWN, USA
123 Incorporated was a small company that was bought out by 789 Corporation in 2005.

STAFF ASSOCIATE 9/2002–4/2004

Worked on a variety of projects as assigned using Excel, Word, and database research. Liaised with management and clients regarding content-related issues and supervised interns performing basic Internet research.
- Was selected for company's employee activity committee.

INTERN 5/2002–8/2002

Performed basic Internet research as assigned by staff associates.

EDUCATION

BA – Management, American University, Washington, DC May 2002
Certified Management Accountant, IMA 2005

SKILLS

Oracle Sequel Query, Filenet, Premium Accounting System, Premium Audit Adjustment Module, and Premium Processing System; proficient with Microsoft Office 97 (Excel, Microsoft Word, Access Database), Lotus 1-2-3, and WordPerfect; excellent work ethic, communication skills, and interpersonal skills.

FIVE YEAR UPDATE (2013)

Susie Smith, MBA
555 Any Street
Anytown, USA 00000
(555) 555-5555
Susie_Smith@whateveremail.com

OBJECTIVE

To find a position in executive senior management that offers a wide variety of challenges and responsibilities in a major corporation.

WORK EXPERIENCE

1/2007–present
ABC Company, Anytown, USA
ABC Company is a $2B publicly traded international manufacturing company.

Executive Vice President-International Division 1/2010 to present
Supervise all activities of $1B international division with one hundred direct reports in eighteen countries. Report directly to COO. Responsibilities include overseeing all aspects of operations including sales, distribution, human resources, and manufacturing.

- Made internal operational improvements that increased profits from operations by 35% over two consecutive periods.
- Received outstanding inventory audit results with less than .5% loss due to shrinkage.
- Had 100% success in eliminating job site injuries for eighteen consecutive months.
- Reduced staff turnover to less than 5% annually by implementing long-term bonus pay plan.
- Was promoted from vice president to executive vice president 1/2013.

Division Manager 1/2008–12/2010
Managed staff of five in the domestic distribution division, a $500M division. Reported to divisional director. Responsibilities included hiring, training, and mentoring of staff in accordance with company guidelines. Maintained divisional reporting and ensured timely reporting to corporate.

- Received "Top Performance Award 2007" for suggesting and implementing a new procedure that saved the company over $15,000 in printing costs.
- Implemented new employee referral program and reduced turnover to less than 10% in under six months.

Senior Associate 1/2007–1/2008
Responsibilities included monitoring the activities of the distribution center including production, error reporting, and quality control activities. Reported to division manager and was promoted into that position after the manager's departure.

- Was selected as "Associate of the Month" four times in 2007

5/2004–12/2006
XYZ Partners, Anytown, USA
XYZ Partners is a privately held company with 2,000 employees in six states.

Senior Associate 8/2005–12/2006
Responsibilities included assisting in training and supervision of three staff associates performing word processing and proofreading as assigned. Ensured quality control guidelines and project deadlines were being met. Reported to senior manager of production.
- Was chosen to work on prestigious project for member of Congress requiring security and background screening.

Staff Associate 5/2004–7/2005
Received job-specific training on document control and word processing as required by diverse clientele. Position required attention to detail, accuracy, and strong computer skills using Word. Reported to senior associate and was promoted into that role.
- Discovered and corrected major data entry error that ultimately made the database run twice as efficiently.

5/2002–4/2004
123 Incorporated, New Town, USA
123 Incorporated was a small company that was bought out by 789 Corporation in 2005.

Staff Associate 9/2002–4/2004
Worked on a variety of projects as assigned using Excel, Word and database research. Liaised with management and clients regarding content-related issues and supervised interns performing basic Internet research.
- Was selected for company's employee activity committee.

Intern 5/2002-8/2002
Performed basic Internet research as assigned by staff associates.

EDUCATION AND CERTIFICATIONS
MBA - Northwestern University, Chicago, IL Dec. 2010
BA – Management, American University, Washington, DC May 2002
Certified Management Accountant, IMA 2005

SKILLS
Oracle Sequel Query, Filenet, Premium Accounting System, Premium Audit Adjustment Module, and Premium Processing System; proficient with Microsoft Office 97 (Excel, Microsoft Word, Access Database), Lotus 1-2-3, and WordPerfect; excellent work ethic, communication skills, and interpersonal skills.

TEN EASY STEPS TO A PERFECT RESUME

STEP ONE: KEEP YOUR LAYOUT SIMPLE AND MAKE SURE YOUR CONTACT INFORMATION IS ACCURATE AND CORRECT.

STEP TWO: ADD THE COMPANIES YOU HAVE WORKED FOR AND THE DATES YOU WORKED THERE.

STEP THREE: ADD A QUICK DESCRIPTION OF THE COMPANY.

STEP FOUR: ADD YOUR JOB DESCRIPTIONS.

STEP FIVE: ADD YOUR ACCOMPLISHMENTS.

STEP SIX: FORMATTING THE PAGE.

STEP SEVEN: ADDING EDUCATION AND CERTIFICATIONS.

STEP EIGHT: ADDING SKILLS.

STEP NINE: EVALUATE YOUR CONTENT AND CREATE AN OBJECTIVE.

STEP TEN: PROOFREAD YOUR COMPLETED CONTENT.

ACKNOWLEDGEMENTS

I owe numerous debts of gratitude to many people for their support and encouragement over the years. In particular I'd like to thank those people directly involved with the publication of this book:

My loving husband, James, for being a constant source of support and an excellent editor.

My immediate family and friends for their encouragement and feedback. For those family, friends and colleagues no longer with us: you are missed but never forgotten.

All the candidates I have worked on resumes with: per your requests I have finally put our work into writing!

All my clients I have served: your feedback on the resumes I have sent over the years made this book possible.

Gail Cato for being an amazing editor. Your input was invaluable.

Dave Singleton for being a fantastic collaborator and friend.

My Pinnacle Society colleagues: I find inspiration in each of you and am grateful to you all for helping me find my voice.

My old bosses particularly Henry Rienstra, Eric Olson and Brad Violette: You each impacted me in so many positive ways I can't thank you enough.

My past and present co-workers, employees and business partners: I appreciate all that you do and have done for me particularly Courtnie Cho, Mimi Tom, Scott Kesler, Bill Wright, Susan Gallagher and last but not least, Sabrina Telles for her hours of assistance with the exhibits.

AUTHOR BIO

Carolyn Thompson resides in the Washington, DC area and has been an executive recruiter since 1988. Carolyn is a creative entrepreneur and a certified career coach. She is frequently called upon by national news organizations such as **The Washington Post, The Wall Street Journal, and NPR** among others to contribute content on a variety of topics. Her articles on career development, executive coaching, recruiting and the employment industry have been published in various national magazines, trade journals, and on the Internet. An enthusiastic motivational speaker, she is a member of the Pinnacle Society* and the International Coach Federation**.

Carolyn is an alumnus of Kansas State University and author of TEN EASY STEPS TO A PERFECT RESUME and TEN STEPS TO FINDING THE PERFECT JOB, now available in select bookstores and on Amazon.com.

Look for her upcoming title, TEN SECRETS TO GETTING PROMOTED.

Her blog can be found at www.JobSearchJungle.com.

For more information on job search, recruiting, staffing, and executive search visit www.CM-CS.com

For more information on executive coaching, sales, and recruiter training visit www.CarolynThompson.net

*www.pinnaclesociety.org   *The Pinnacle Society is the nation's premier consortium of top recruiters within the permanent placement industry. Since 1989, membership is limited to 75 of the nation's top recruiters.*

**www.coachfederation.org   *The International Coach Federation is the largest worldwide resource for business and personal coaches.*